THE BLACK CHURCH HERITAGE

An African American Case Study
in Dixon, Illinois

Rev. Dr. Larry Jones, Ph.D.

GlobalEdAdvance
Press

THE BLACK CHURCH HERITAGE

AN AFRICAN AMERICAN CASE STUDY IN DIXON, ILLINOIS

Copyright © 2009, 2021 by Larry Jones

Library of Congress Control Number: 2009921755

ISBN 978-1-935434-34-4

Subject Codes and Description:

1: SOC001000: Social Science: African – Ethical Studies-African American; 2. SOC039000: Social Science: Sociology of Religion; 3. REL012110 Religion: Christian Life- Social

All rights reserved, including the right to reproduce this book or any part thereof in any form, except for inclusion of brief quotations in a review, without the written permission of the author and GlobalEdAdvance Press.

Cover by GlobalGraphics

City of Publication: Nashville, TN

Printed in Australia, Brazil, EU, France, Germany, Italy, Poland, Russia, Spain, UK (3 sites in USA) and available on the Espresso Book Machine© worldwide.

The Press does not have ownership of the contents of a book; this is the author's work and the author owns the copyright. All theory, concepts, constructs, and perspectives are those of the author and not necessarily the Press. They are presented for open and free discussion of the issues involved. All comments and feedback should be directed to the Email: [comments4author@aol.com] and the comments will be forwarded to the author for response.

Published by

GlobalEdAdvancePRESS

GlobalEdAdvance.org

Order books from www.gea-books.com/bookstore/
or any place good books are sold.

This book is dedicated to

Jennifer, my wife
and
Zaneta & Victoria, my daughters.

Thank you for your love
and support.

Contents

Preface:
    A Divine Emancipation   9

Introduction:
    A Segregated Sunday Morning   29

1	The Black Church Experience	37
2	The African American Settlers in Dixon	47
3	The Early Black Baptist	53
4	The Early Methodist Movement	61
5	The Additional Methodist Center	69
6	The Prison Ministry Involvement	75
7	The Fight for Justice Continues	81

About the Author   89

Appendix One:
    Book Logo Data   91

Appendix Two:
    The Commonality of the Golden Rule   95

Appendix Three:
    Sources Listed By Date   97

Amazing grace! (how sweet the sound)That sav'd a wretch like me! I once was lost, but now am found, was blind, but now I see.

—John Newton

Preface

A Divine Emancipation

An Amazing Deliverance

John Newton, master of a slave ship, encountered a divine emancipation he called his "great deliverance," after praying during a storm at sea (1748). Continuing in the slave trade after this experience, he began to change his attitude and slaves under his care were treated humanely. Yet this change was not sufficient to satisfy a changed heart. He returned home, became a minister in the Church of England and wrote many religious songs. For a weekly service Newton wrote "amazing grace" and sang it to a tune he learned by the humming of slaves. The first publication of Amazing Grace was in 1779 three decades after his life-changing experience.

Social change comes slowly. The John Newton story is of a changed man who delayed positive action. It took a long time for him to change an agenda and act appropriately. After his heart was changed, his mind developed in a spiritual direction, and eventually he was able to execute positive acts toward the people he had wronged. His words and music still speak volumes today for anyone who will listen. This provides hope that positive and constructive change will come. The question is "Where, when and with whom will it begin?" Try closing your eyes and humming the tune to Amazing Grace: it can change your life.

Individuals Can Change

In social theory one learns that individuals change more rapidly than groups; groups faster than communities; communities easier than society. An affirmative attitude is needed to make a drastic difference, but legislation for groups of people is not the objective. Individuals are the persons who can change. Leadership is the ability to influence others to follow one toward stated objectives. It is influence that changes individuals and changed individuals are able to influence group change. Then, small groups with an altered mindset can change the communities of which they are apart. Eventually, society will feel the force of gradual positive change. When it is gradual change overtime, social change will be accepted and even embraced. Most prefer instant change, but social change is sequential and incremental overtime. Patience is required.

False Human Barriers to Social Progress

This hopeful anticipation is based on the social theory timetable, but it should be remembered that discrimination and slavery did not begin with the American Colonies or the Southern Confederacy. This inequity and bigotry began in the wicked hearts and money-oriented minds of civilized men around the world who chose to abandon moral values and merchandise in African slaves. Perceiving themselves to be superior, this racial discrimination and bigotry built legal fences and social walls creating false human barriers to social progress. Some remnants of discrimination remain that perpetuate roadblocks to shared human advancement. Yet there were converts.

Lincoln and Grant Must be Given Credit

Segregation in the United States began centuries ago before America was a Nation. In the decade of the 1860's, America fought a Civil War and President Lincoln signed the Emancipation Proclamation to free all in servitude. On March 30, 1870 the Fifteenth Amendment was ratified: "The rights of citizens of the United States to vote shall not be denied or abridged by the United States or any State on account of race, color, or previous condition of servitude." The following day, May 31, 1870 President Ulysses S. Grant signed the first Enforcement Act that substantially secured the voting rights of freedmen. One year later, President Grant signed the Second Enforcement Act (1871) to protect black suffrage and targeted the activities of violent groups that resisted the progress. About five years later, President Grant signed the Civil Rights Act of 1875. This groundbreaking act prohibited segregation in various modes of public accommodations and transportation and discrimination in jury selection.

Action Unsurpassed in Presidential History

President Grant's role in securing the full political equality of all Americans regardless of race is unsurpassed in presidential history. Even after the popular will overwhelmingly turned against the President's efforts to protect the political and civil rights of former slaves, Ulysses S. Grant refused to abandon his commitment to those for whose freedom he had fought. After he left office, the federal government allowed the South to enter a new era of segregation and disfranchisement. During this period, President Grant's efforts to protect the freedmen during Reconstruction were widely ridiculed and declared to be misguided. Such criticism, however, has crumbled in the face of history.

The Kennedy/Johnson Effort

About 100 years later, despite President Kennedy's assassination (1963), his proposal culminated in the Civil Rights Act of 1964. President Lyndon Johnson is given credit for pushing the Civil Rights Act through Congress. Progress has been made with minorities in Cabinet positions and in elected office across the nation. The Inauguration of Barak Obama (January 20, 2009) as the 44th President of the United States of America was a major step in removing the social guilt of the American people.

A Footnote to History

A footnote to this historical event: it should be noted that Black Men received the right to vote before Women did. Black men were "symbolically" given the right to vote in 1870 with the 15th amendment, but in reality most did not vote out of fear and intimidation by the white establishment. Women on the other hand gained the right to vote in 1920 with the 19th amendment. Difficulties with voter registration and the use of a poll tax which was not lifted until 1964 with the 24th amendment. The Voting Rights Act of 1975 finally gave black men the free opportunity to vote. Could this be the reason people turned to Candidate Obama instead of Mrs. Clinton? Perhaps the next President will be a woman. With patience and tolerance, conceivably within a decade or two the United States of America will develop a color blind society and begin to function as a melting pot rather than a stew pot.

A Social Change Timetable

Everyone is in a hurry to make constructive changes, but reality must be faced squarely. Haste makes waste. It takes as long to solve a social problem as it took to create the problem in the first place. Some gender, racial, ethnic, religious, and national origin issues have been with society for hundreds of years. Does this mean constructive change can never happen in one lifetime? Of course, not! However, understanding the social theory does assist the appreciation for the small changes one sees and increases the tolerance for the gradual improvements that are taking place. Is the change moving fast enough? Of course, not! Again, the process can be nudged a little, but it cannot be pushed beyond the norms of a social change timetable.

Constructive Social Change

Constructive social change does not come easy. Community leaders must make a contextual analysis of the population by looking at every aspect of the community. When the people are viewed as a whole one sees a different picture than when community is broken down into parts: cultures, traditions, ethnic groups, business organizations, government personnel, religious institutions, social clubs, medical facilities, and institutions of learning. Separating a whole into parts assists leaders in determining the nature, proportion, function, and relationship of various aspects of the community in order to weave or knit together a new integrated entity that would demonstrate positive social change.

Affirmative Attitude Required

A minority cannot protect itself against the violence imposed by discrimination, injustice, or prejudice. When choices are made on the basis of gender, race, religion, ethnic origin or lifestyle rather than on core values and character, little can be done without external forces coming to the rescue. Internal resistance only breeds more expressions of violence and prejudicial behavior. Only a willing majority can honestly protect the minority within a given community, honestly negotiate from strength and have the will to make changes to gain constructive progress. This is not done by laws, but by clear rejection of negative behavior on both sides of the issue and an honest adjustment of attitude. What is needed is not only affirmative action, but an affirmative attitude. Everyone must be seen as a person of worth with a potential productive contribution to the community. Without this attitude, positive social change will never happen.

A Small Difference

Civil Rights Laws and affirmative action made a small difference for some in the level of overt expressions of discrimination and injustice, but not in the core attitude of the majority. There are still those in the majority that either accept the whole and reject the part or accept the part and reject the whole. What is needed is an affirmative attitude toward all people. The articulation of an assenting approach to responsible change, lawful behavior, and the attitude of a good neighbor should come from a positive predisposition to behave responsibly.

A Natural Phenomenon

Normally, a population will accept a minority, an ethnic group, or a social class into the community to the degree the group exists on the national scene. Since people gather in groups according to cultural orientation: food selection, clothing style, music appreciation, spoken language, family religion, political choice, and ethnic background, different groups must be recognized and viewed based on their function in the community. When a single group grows beyond the national norm in a given community, others begin to show favoritism and express prejudice.

Discrimination has a Life of its Own

Discrimination at first is a natural occurrence, but as crime, loss of jobs, and negative personal encounters increase more disapproving feelings are expressed. It then begins to take on a life of its own and grows exponentially until violence beaks out. Laws, housing and school zoning, highway and street constructions or similar efforts to fence in a minority cannot stop the growing feelings of anger. Prejudice, bigotry, and narrow mindedness are normally learned in the home, not on the streets. The family unit is the key to understanding discrimination. It would be good if everyone could accept the family next door and across the street as part of the community. It would be great if whole families could communicate as the younger children do.

Internal Redirection of Attitudes

This level of communication will not happen until there is an internal redirection of attitudes at home; it will not happen until parents and older siblings behave responsibly and become examples of good citizens.

However, individuals cannot change by themselves. Normally, it takes an outside force such as, religion, community recreation, political fairness, or just plain good and honest behavior to affect such change. It may take a drastic readjustment of the psyche or redemption of the spirit to make a major adjustment to the subconscious attitude of the heart and generate a willingness to behave responsibly.

Limits of Normal Social Change

Part of the problem is that minority groups have raised their expectations beyond the limits of normal social change. Also, some of the majority have either stuck their heads in the sand or dug their heels in the dirt. Higher levels of change would require a drastic and costly revolution such as the Civil War. Tolerance must be taught, demonstrated, and lived daily in the community to prepare for constructive change. Discrimination must be condemned and punished. Honesty and fairness must control all relationships. Then, an only then, can a pluralistic community live in peace and comfort with neighbors at the family table next door or across the street. It is coming; be patient.

A Forgiving Spirit

Patience is a virtue in social change. It is the ability to remain under pressure with a positive attitude until relief comes. That is why the Ancient Greeks called the sick folk who came to see a physician "patients," because they had to remain under the pressure of illness until the medical practitioner was able to treat the infirmity. Patience means a calm endurance of hardship, inconvenience or delay until better conditions arrive. Patience is identified by tolerance of a situation that is unacceptable; it is developed by misfortune and suffering, strengthened by enduring the present, magnified by uncomplaining hope, and characterized by a forgiving spirit directed toward those who resist change.

Roadblocks

Some members of the minority have personally risen above the fray and been assisted over the wall and through the maze to a better life, but some individuals in minorities have been hindered in their personal and social progress. Some of the roadblocks have been within conservative politics, the religious community, inside community leadership, and sometimes within the minority itself.

Some said Sunday morning was the most segregated hour of the week in America. Perhaps this is true, but is it by coercion or choice? When social integration works in education, housing, and the work place, why is Sunday morning still segregated? Could it be by choice based on cultural (Black) heritage?

One of my graduate students at Oxford Graduate School did a study to determine the impact of social integration on the survival of Southern Black Community-based organizations. When three indices were compared (Social Integration Index, Black Community-based organization Participation Index, and Black Heritage Index), the level of social integration made no difference in community-based organization participation. Only the Black Heritage Index made a significant difference. The higher the Black Heritage Index the greater the probability of participation in ethnic-based worship. It was not segregation, but cultural heritage that drew them to the religious activities and the music that fulfilled their cultural needs.

So it is possible for a minority group to be integrated socially, economically, and educationally and still maintain ethnic-based activities. After all most of the local community-based organizations and all the denominations in America have a cultural control indicator. This is not a justification for Sunday segregation, but an explanation of how it has happened. In fact it is the minorities who continue this participation as part of a cultural and heritage expression. As long as ethnicity survives there will be ethnic-based activities. This will gradually change overtime, but it will change on its own, not by external forces or even gentle persuasion.

Integrated into the Social Fabric

As the essential elements of personal faith, not sectarian dogma, are integrated into the social fabric of a community, there will be gradual social change. Only a drastic transformation of the heart or a spiritual renewal of the soul could speed up the process. Heritage and tradition are big components of social resistance to change. Heritage becomes a legacy passed on by tradition to the next generation. At times it may be perpetuated by inheritance factors when family elders have traditionally been associated with a particular institution or ethnic-based activity/experience, the young may feel obligated or privileged to follow the same path. Most want to hold on to the memories and the subconscious imprinting of the past. The more this difficulty is understood, the better society will be in accepting the gradual social change that is predictable.

Sectarian Positions

A cultural framework for establishing sectarian positions has been the norm in Christianity. Some American groups developed congregations out of the historical and cultural conditions of the American scene. The congregations of the (Christian) Restoration Movement and such groups as the Holiness and Pentecostal Movements are examples. It seems that cultural foundations can identify most, if not all American denominational groups. These cultural and regional origins have colored various interpretations of Scripture and transformed tradition into cultural barriers. Over time these various interpretations of sectarian teachings were given brand names and promoted as the correct and proper way to worship and find peace, happiness, and eternal life.

Cultural Roots or National Origins

Most religious groups and divisions can be traced to cultural roots or national origins. The Roman Catholic identity is obvious. The Community-based organization of England, the Greek and Russian Orthodox Churches have obvious national influence. Methodist and Episcopal congregations have English beginnings, Presbyterians have Scottish roots, Lutherans have foundations in Germany, Baptists have European beginnings, and the list goes on. At one time in America, there was even a Swedish Baptist Church. This particular group changed its identity when it ran out of Swedes. American religious groups have created congregations clustered around sectarian constructs with brand names that have identified and advanced a particular perspective as an accurate interpretation of scripture. When the young are taught these traditions, it is difficult to make meaningful change or produce a spirit of cooperation among the various divisions in the community of faith.

Cultural Glasses

Scripture, which is supposed to be the Word of God for all people, has been viewed through cultural glasses and the private interpretations differ from group to group. Consequently, universal truth became the exclusive domain of a particular religious authority and limited to a selected doctrinal or sectarian constituency. Various teachings and different doctrine were culturally interpreted but firmly and authoritatively proclaimed as the true and proper expression of the inspired scriptural writings. While Judaism, the Roman Catholics, and members of Islam have differences, a unified message is presented to the world. The Christian community accentuates differences as a badge of honor. Each group behaving as if they have found the "Holy Grail" and have exclusive access to the "secrets" of faith and practice. This facilitates the religious segregation in America and encourages division within families and communities.

American Judaism has small internal differences, but the Jewish community maintains a unified identity. When individuals are identified as being Jewish, one immediately has an idea of their basic values. Judaism has a sense of community and commitment to the individual and family. The public understands much of the essential elements of Jewish worship and family values.

Although some differences exist among Roman Catholics, they manage to present a unified voice to the average American citizen. Other sectarian groups, such as Mormons, Jehovah Witnesses, or Islam manage to overcome differences and present a common identity. This is not true of most Protestant communions in America. This greatly complicates the integration of moral principles into society. "Can two walk together except they agree?" Some of these basic moral principles and religious experiences would enhance the acceptance among minorities and greatly advance caring for one's neighbor and loving one another in true acts of common humanity, but human nature perpetuates division and conflict. No wonder the American church is failing to reach the next generation.

Identified and Branded

American Protestants are not presently identified as "Christian," but as Baptist, Methodist, Lutheran, Pentecostal, Presbyterian, and the list goes on and on. This has become name-brand religion in the eyes of the community. As if this were not enough division, multiple identities and doctrines exist within each of these sectarian groups. Is this a result of the pluralism in America, and an inevitable consequence of an immigrant nation? Can American Christians not lay aside small traditional differences and develop a unified identity around common tenets? Are there no converts to the Christian Faith, just adherents to sectarian dogma? Must each individual who embraces a community of faith be branded and identified as free-range cattle belonging to a particular ranch or rancher? Must one belong to a particular political party to favor positive social change?

These differences are based on culture, tradition, and language, not on firm spiritual or exegetical grounds. Most scholars know these facts, but the community is turned off by the confused and muddled message. Constructive change is possible, but to affect such change there must be true change of heart and the lessening of sectarian dogma. There must be more than an intellectual apprehension of facts; there must be acceptance of truth that can change hearts and lives. Otherwise, religion will have less influence on the community in the Twenty-first Century than in the past and communities will remain divided, segregated, separated, isolated, and not relevant to the present generation.

A Stained-Glass Barrier

Sectarian groups meetings on Sunday have created a stained-glass barrier between the community and between religious groups with almost sameness of belief. Small cultural and traditional procedures continue to separate religious groups into a kind of franchise system. These divisions have become a barrier to the larger social integration of the community. These divisions became the building blocks of a cultural and communication barrier between the sacred and the secular communities. Some sectarian groups are not willing to alter religious vocabulary to understandable terms for the general public; consequently, they become a barrier to social change.

Freeze-Frame Thinking

Early religious gatherings did not have a bound, printed document to argue over the parsing of Greek words or disagree over the grammatical description of a word or group of words. The early believers had an experiential relationship with a Person and enjoyed genuine fellowship with each other. The Bible is a relational book and is filled with attitudes to be caught, rather than doctrines to be taught. If these attitudes were practiced, leaders would discard name-brand religion that confuses society and freeze frame theology that divides the groups. Without agreement they cannot walk on the same path. If the churches were together on the little issues, perhaps Christians could get together on the big issue of segregation, justice, and discrimination. This freeze frame thinking has created a barrier to contemporary morality and values. Since constructive social change and integration take place at the level of ideas and values, ideology is the common ground of application and integration of the moral and ethical mindset in society. What is your mindset?

What are you willing to do?

Most Christians have forgotten that it was a man of Africa, Simon of Cyrene, a passer-by who was compelled by Roman Soldiers to carry the Cross of Jesus up to the place of Crucifixion on Calvary. Simon had two sons, Alexander and Rufus (Mark 15.21). They became leaders in the church. Some have forgotten that Dr. Martin Luther King, Jr. bravely carried the Civil Rights cross up the American Hill of Difficulty to his own death. His children have continued the struggle. What are you willing to do to make a difference in your community? Will you help someone carry their cross? Will you stand firm for the rights of others? One man - one vote can make a difference!

Hollis L. Green, ThD, PhD
Distinguished Professor of
Education and Social Change

The vote is the most powerful instrument ever devised by man for breaking down injustice and destroying the terrible walls which imprison men because they are different from other men.

— John Fitzgerald Kennedy

Nonviolence is a powerful and just
weapon. It is a weapon unique in history,
which cuts without wounding and
ennobles the man who wields it.
It is a sword that heals.

— Martin Luther King, Jr.

Introduction

A Segregated Sunday Morning

The segregated Sunday morning forced African Americans to form their own churches. This further perpetuated the divisions in the community. The problem of Social Integration has suggested that it would hinder the viability of the Black Church. However, the factor that is most determinative is the level of Black Heritage. Provided an adequate level of Black Heritage, exists most people of color can feel comfortable in any church.

Why Did This Happen?

It seems that the North and the South looked at segregation from different perspectives. In the Deep South the facts suggest that people of color were rejected as a whole, but accepted as individuals. Above the Mason Dixon Line the facts suggest the opposite. It appears that with all the big talk about being different from the Deep South, it was just talk. People of color were publicly accepted as a whole, but privately rejected at the individual level. This difference made the segregation of the North that discriminated against individuals much more troublesome than the practice of the South. Although the race was rejected as a whole, on an individual basis and at the individual level people were respected. This is what Dr. King meant when he spoke often about "accepting individuals on the basis of their character rather than on the color of their skin." The story of Dixon, Illinois is not much different than other parts of the country where people of color were made to feel that their "place" was in a segregated church on Sunday morning.

Was Sunday Morning Wasted?

When there is an absence of Christian charity and personal respect for the rights and feelings of others, it seems a travesty to come to a place of worship and pretend that God is love and everything is right with the world. What happened to the Golden Rule? Where was social equality? What about the founding fathers statement "All men being created equal?" Has the American church won the world for Christ? Did God prosper the efforts to advance missions when the attitudes at home prohibited the reaching of individuals in the same community? No wonder Sunday morning was considered a wasted time by the American Press in 1957.

Editors of popular *Look* magazine shocked the church world with a 1957 cover story, "Sunday school: most wasted hour of the week?" Their question came after surveying people who had been to Sunday school for years and yet had almost no biblical literacy, theological foundation or definitive doctrine. *Look's* conclusion was, "Sunday School is the only school in the world that is not a school." Protestant leaders admitted that no failure of the American churches had been greater than that of the Sunday School. However, I beg to differ.

The great failure was to claim a missionary spirit, yet segregate people of color. Sending missionaries and funds to places such as Africa, but denying access of African Americans to their churches at home. The greatest, however, was to permit the church to be segregated on Sunday morning. This sent a strong message to society and delayed the process of integration. Even where it was "legal" for integrated services, most people of color felt out of place and preferred to be in their "place" with people who loved and respected them as individuals and their culture.

Dr. Martin Luther King, Jr., once said, "11:00 a.m. on a Sunday morning is the most segregated place in America." A tragic fact of the American church is that Sunday morning can commonly be known as "the most segregated hour of the week." This means that Sunday morning worship services at local churches most clearly demonstrate both the racial divide and social divisions that exists in most cities and towns across America. People go where they are comfortable and unfortunately that does not include church. White people go to their church; black people attend their church, rich people go to church with other rich people, and educated people go to church with other educated people. Styles of worship are different. Ideally, all people who call themselves Christian should go into any church and feel as if they belong, but that is not the case in Dixon, Illinois or in many other cities of America.

During the 1960s, the majority of churches and most places of business were segregated. Consequently, a movement began in the United States to bring integration to all aspects of society. Churches were no exception. However, protesting segregation in the church was controversial. Some felt that they had the right to worship as they pleased with whomever they pleased, while others thought it was hypocritical of the church to deny membership to certain people because of their race. In order to protest this form of segregation, many people staged "kneel–ins," so called because people would kneel outside the churches in prayer as a peaceful protest. These "kneel-ins" occurred in churches of all denominations, but became more popular as the Civil Rights Movement gained momentum around 1963.

"Kneel-ins" typically began with an interracial group of college age students choosing seven or eight churches to attend. The churches they chose had all-white membership and were typically large, influential churches in the community. The majority of the time the visitors were welcomed into the service; however, "kneel-ins" occurred at the churches that would not allow the interracial groups to attend service.

A pastor normally organized the protests and led these interracial groups of students. Organizations such as the NAACP or the Student Non-Violent Coordinating Commission (SNCC) also arranged to have groups of students attend protests at local churches. Protestors came from all over the country, and many came to witness first-hand the Civil Rights Movement.

When the interracial groups arrived at churches, church elders or ushers normally denied them admittance by meeting them at the door and telling them they were not welcome. Churches began to hire guards to stand outside the doors and control those who tried to enter the church. It was also common for the ushers or church elders to deny these groups access to the church, and challenge the pastors, who supported integration

In fact, many of these churches had no specific written rules against African Americans worshiping at their church; however, the members felt the rule was "implied." When denied admittance to the service, many of the groups of students would kneel in prayer or sit outside and read the Bible, which is how these protests received the name "kneel-ins" or "pray-ins". Those who decided to stay and participate in a "kneel-in" and did not vacate the church property, were threatened with arrest, and in some cases were arrested.

President Carter had Difficulty

President Jimmy Carter had some difficulty with the press and others when he attempted to explain the diversity of the American population. Carter expressed a belief that life was not always fair, and argued for the right of different cultural and racial groups to maintain their ethnicity. Scholars agree with President Carter that the music, art, language, food, clothing, and other aspects of ethnic culture and religious expression are important to each group. Ancestry, history, and social background are all a part of one's heritage. Americans are proud of both their heritage and their differences. These make the United States of America a strong and viable democracy. The big question: Why do religious leaders, who are enjoined to even "love their enemies" and to "pray for those who despitefully use them", not find strength in the common elements of diversity? Why can they not agree to disagree agreeably and move forward with a common message?

After his years as Governor of Georgia and four years in the Presidency, the Carters moved back to the small town they called home. He was disappointed that his home church in Georgia was still practicing the segregated Sunday morning. With great difficulty he attempted to rectify the situation, but was unable to change the hard core group that insisted on the old ways. Consequently, the Carters with great anguish of spirit forsook their home church and started attending a new church that welcomed people of all races. If more individuals would stand up to the bigotry more progress could be made. Meanwhile, the struggle continues in many parts of the USA.

> We are confronted primarily with
> a moral issue… whether all Americans
> are to be afforded equal rights and
> equal opportunities, whether we are
> going to treat our fellow Americans
> as we want to be treated.
>
> —John Fitzgerald Kennedy

1

The Black Church Experience

The Dixon Community proper has forty (40) Churches with four small churches serving the African Community: Although there are more churches in the Area of Dixon on the Chamber of Commerce List. The distribution of churches seems to be along population and ethnic lines. The highest number of churches relate to the make up of the population. There are five Catholic Churches, four Baptist Churches, four Lutheran Churches, three Community Churches and two Black Churches and one of these considers itself integrated.

- Alliance Churches (1)
- Assembly of God Churches (1)
- Baptist Churches (4)
- Brethren Churches (2)

- Catholic Churches (5)
- Christian Churches (2)
- Church of God Churches (1)
- Community Churches (3)
- Congregational Churches (1
- Disciples of Christ Churches (1)
- Episcopal Churches (1)
- Evangelical Churches (2)
- Foursquare Gospel Churches (1)
- Full Gospel Churches (1)
- Independent Churches (1)
- Jehovah's Witness Churches (1
- Lutheran Churches (4)
- Methodist Churches (2)
- Mission Churches (1)
- Non-Denominational Churches (2)
- Presbyterian Churches (1)
- Pentecostal Churches (1)
- United Methodist Churches (1)

Black History Month

Dr. Carter Godwin Woodson, the Father of Black History Month now celebrated in February, believed that all African Americans should know their past in order to participate in the affairs of their country. Dr. Woodson, born to former slave parents, wrote extensively about the accomplishments of Blacks in America. According to Dr. Woodson, "African Americans have excelled in areas of Sports, Education, Literature, Science, Business, Medicine, and Civil Rights, but the greatest of their accomplishment has been in the institution of the church."

Black church history can be traced back into numerous areas of diverse antiquity. It was the church that explained the tedious pilgrimage of Black sons and daughters of Africa into a land known as North America. The church redefined America's view of "blackness" by elevating it from a repugnant and repelling state to a resilient and compelling status that symbolized spirituality, courage, triumph, and success. It is therefore evident why the church is the most influential institution in the African American community. The church has inspired individuals to overcome extraordinary hardships and hurdles.

During the early black church experiences in America, seven major denominations emerged: The African Methodist Episcopal Church (AMEC), The African Methodist Episcopal Zion Church (AMEZ), The

Christian Methodist Episcopal Church (CMEC), The Church of God in Christ (COGIC), The National Baptist Convention, USA, Incorporated (NBC), The National Baptist Convention of America, Unincorporated (NBCA) and The Progressive National Baptist Convention (PNBC). As such, distinguished clergymen emerged to become the focal point for their com-munity. Martin de Porres was the Catholic Church's first mulatto Saint. August Talton was the first African American Catholic Priest. James Healy was the first African American Catholic Bishop. Thomas Paul brought independence to the black Baptist. John Jasper preached to a mixed congregation regarding the inherent evils of slavery.

From the era of American slavery through the Civil Rights movement of the 1960's, black clergy consistently taught that racial hatred and violence was a threat to the foundation of human dignity and humanity. Those same clergymen also taught that our destiny was not in the hands of a dominant racial group, but in the hand of a sovereign God.

Leaders of the Civil Rights Movement

The leaders of the Civil Rights Movement were Black Clergy. This fact caused some to question the validity of the struggle. What if these preachers are successful in their effort to bring total integration to America? What if they succeed in eliminating the Segregated Sunday morning? What would happen to the Black Church in the South? The real question was: if one were integrated in housing, education, the workplace, and somewhat socially, would they want to attend a Black Church on Sunday morning?

Black Heritage Index Made the Difference

Dr. Robert L. Allen, was the pastor of Zion Baptist Church in Chattanooga, Tennessee in 1987. He became concerned about the viability of the Black Church in the south and did a study to determine the impact of social integration on the survival of Southern Black Churches entitled "The Impact of Social Integration on the Black Church of Chattanooga, Tennessee." When three indices were compared (Social Integration Index, Black Church Participation Index, and Black Heritage Index), the level of social integration made no difference in Black Church participation in the cases studies. Only the Black Heritage Index made a significant difference. The higher the Black Heritage Index the greater the probability of participation in ethnic-based worship regardless of the level of social integrations.

Dr. Allen determined that it was not segregation, but cultural heritage that drew people of color to the religious activities and the music that fulfilled their cultural needs. So it is possible for a minority group to be integrated socially, economically, and educationally and still maintain Black Church activities. After all most of the local churches and all the denominations in America have a cultural control indicator. This is not a justification for Sunday segregation, or an effort to justify racial bigotry, but an explanation of how it has happened. Although one should not generalize the findings of Dr. Allen's research in Chattanooga, Tennessee to the whole of the Black Church in America, it does point to a possible explanation as to why some ethnic groups prefer to worship within their own tradition.

There is nothing fundamentally wrong with Black people worshipping in a predominately Black church when this participation is part of a cultural and heritage expression. The problem is when others attempt by both overt and/or covert means to create an atmosphere the leads to the segregated Sunday morning. As long as ethnicity survives there will be some ethnic-based activities. This will gradually change overtime, but it will change on its own, not by external forces or even gentle persuasion. There are hopeful signs in the politics of America. Cultural change is coming, but it cannot be pushed; it must be a natural development based on an affirmative attitude rather than just affirmative action.

If Germanic people wish to attend a Lutheran Church or people of Irish or Italian decent prefer the Catholic approach to worship, or White Anglo Saxon Protestants (WASP) want to worship in an English or European tradition, so be it. This means that individuals of African decent with a sense of their own Black Heritage who willingly choose to worship with the Black Community should feel comfortable with their ethnicity. However, it does not mean that anyone should refuse the right of others to worship freely anywhere they choose. No one has the right to intimidate other ethnic groups who wish to change their perspective of worship and participate in religious activities other than their ethnic or national origin. Would society permit an individual of German descent to be required to attend a Lutheran Church if a Presbyterian Church was preferred? What about a Jewish individual who desired to convert to Christ-ianity, would that person be told you cannot attend this church because you are Jewish? What if President Obama was told because your father was a Muslim you cannot attend a Christian Church? Political correctness would explode and many who have restricted the participation of the Black community would be outraged.

    Surely there is a better way for honest and God-fearing Americans to behave with regard to people of different ethnic background or different religious traditions. Surely God is color-blind! If most people were fair about race, they would consider that all mankind came out of Africa and that climate, culture, traditions, and centuries of time determined much of what is now considered different about people. In fact there is only one race: the human race created by God.

All Descended from One Origin

    All of mankind is descended from one origin or stock. Regardless of difference in complexion, features, or language, yet they are derived from a common parent. (Acts 17:26) The word blood is often used to denote "race, stock, or kindred." Scripture affirms that all the human family is descended from the same ancestor; consequently, all the variety is to be traced to some cause other than there being different races created. (Genesis 1; Malachi 2:10) St. Paul's affirmation was probably to convince the Greeks that he regarded them all as brethren; that, although he was a Jew by race and now a Christian by religion, yet he was not bound by any narrow notions or prejudices in reference to other people. All are, in this respect, equal and the whole human family, however they may differ in complexion, customs, and laws, are to be regarded and treated as part of a common family. It follows, also, that no one part of the human race has a right to enslave or oppress any other part, on account of difference of complexion or national origin.

Dixon, Illinois is a Religious City

The listing of churches in the Dixon Area by the Chamber of Commerce shows a variety of approaches to worship. This listing demonstrates a broad opportunity for selecting a place of worship. The Worship Center, considers itself to be integrated with both white and black leadership and programs of outreach to the whole community.

The Framers of the Bill of Rights did not purport to "create" rights. Rather, they designed the Bill of Rights to prohibit our Government from infringing rights and liberties presumed to be preexisting.

—Thomas Jefferson

Every segment of our population,
and every individual, has a right to
expect from his government a fair deal.

— Harry S. Truman

2

The African American Settlers in Dixon

John Dixon

Around 1828, Ogee, a man of mixed French and Native American descent, established a ferry and a cabin along the banks of the Rock River. In 1829, an employee of Ogee was named postmaster at the newly constructed post office. John Dixon, the founder, bought Ogee's Ferry in the spring of 1830. Mr. Dixon brought his family to his new establishment on April

11th of the same year. Shortly after, the name of the post office was changed to Dixon's Ferry. The present City of Dixon in Lee County, Illinois has a population of less than 16,000. The city was named for its founder John Dixon.

Two American Presidents are honored in Dixon

Dixon is the site of the Lincoln Monument State Memorial, marking the spot where Abraham Lincoln joined the Illinois militia at Fort Dixon in 1832 during the Black Hawk War.

Dixon was also the boyhood home of the 40th U.S. President, Ronald Reagan. His early home is respected as an important part of the city's history.

The First African Settlers

Peter Hatcher, a prominent African American, was a freed black living in a southern state after the Civil War. It was a difficult time for a black man, even for a freed man. In 1866, a gentleman named Captain John Dysart wanted to give Hatcher a new start in life and offered to relocate and employ him. Peter Hatcher accepted Dysart's offer and moved to Nachusa to be employed under Dysart as a harvest laborer. Presently, Nachusa is a community or township of less than 5,000 in Lee County, in the Dixon metro area. The community name derives from Winnebago for "white haired," the Indians' name for John Dixon.

Peter Hatcher married Jan McGregor. Together they had seven children. His oldest daughter, Bessie, was the first African American to graduate from the Nachusa High School. After graduation, Bessie relocated to the City of Dixon. According to the 1870 Federal Census for Lee County Illinois, among the Africans there were twenty-four males and twelve females living in the City of Dixon at that time.

On March 25, 1899 the Daily Star newspaper printed this story about Hatcher with his African dialect and is presented here as a part of history:

> *While passing through Nachusa recently I was ac-costed by "Uncle" Peter Hatcher, (who is an intelligent colored gentleman of that place), by "How do ye do, sah." After returning his*

salutation I asked him how everything was coming along in the town. "Oh we's doin'frly well, but we don't have de fun we used to hab 35 yea's ago, when Bill and Cap (meaning Capt. Dysart) and some of the others were on the turf. He was a great fellow for fun. I remember one evening he came to me and says, "Pete, some of us is goin' up to Colonel's and swipe some grapes." Well, we got dar soon, but herd a noise, when all skedadled. Jist reached de fence, when whang went a gun and down went Cap. Thought it wouldn't do leab him dar, so dey agreed me bein de strongest, should carry him home and dey put him on my back. He was a big fellow, but I take him cross dat pasture in a hurry.

When I got to de oder side I threw him ober de fence into a ditch, when up he jumped and said, "D------ it, Pete, you pretty near killed me." Well you bet I was surprised; I thought he was dead. I was lame for a week or so after; so was Cap., and I guess Bill was to---- from laughing."

Peter Hatcher died March 24, 1905, he was about seventy years old. His funeral was held at his home and he was buried at the Dunkard Cemetery. In 1915 Mrs. Jan Hatcher died. She had moved away from Nachusa. At her daughter's request her remains were returned to Nachusa and buried next to her husband. Between 1905 and 1915 the cemetery had changed ownership. The Dunkard Cemetery became the Emmert Cemetery. Both. Peter and Jan Hatcher are buried in the Emmert Cemetery, east of Franklin Grove, Illinois, a village in Lee County, in the Dixon metro area.

Lack of Diversity Still Evident

In a city with deep connection to President Ronald Reagan and President Abraham Lincoln, more is needed to foster a better understanding among the African American community. The city should aggressively promote the diversity of all its citizens by following in the footsteps of these and other honored local and national leaders. Visibility of African Americans in the religious community and work force is lacking. The disproportion of African Americans in the criminal justice system is apparent. Working together the city, the churches, the business community, and other institutions can build a stronger and more prosperous community. It is worth the effort!

3

The Early Black Baptist

Second Baptist Church is listed with the Dixon, Illinois Chamber of Commerce

The Second Baptist Church theology is consistent with the teachings of the Baptist faith. The Baptist church originated from within the Protestant separatist movement, a movement which arose in Europe with the goal of breaking away from the Church of England. The early Baptist movement is traced back to 1609 in Amsterdam, and John Smith was one of its first Pastors. The group's embracement of the "believers' baptism" theology became the Baptist's defining movement, and this movement led to the establishment of the first Baptist church.

On March 15, 1843, Dick Gray was born into slavery. Gray was owned by one Indiana Dixon from Noxubee County, Mississippi. After the Civil War, in 1855, Dick Gray proudly changed his name to Richard Henry Boyd. On December 19, 1869, Boyd was baptized into the membership of the Hopewell Baptist Church located in Navasota, Texas. Shortly after his conversion, Boyd acknowledged his calling into the preaching ministry. Boyd became a preacher, missionary, entrepreneur, publisher, banker, educator, writer, and Black Nationalist, and one of the early pioneers in the Black Baptist Church.

After attending a Baptist convention in 1872, Boyd felt that the black voice of the convention was not being heard. Boyd, along with a few other ministers, broke away from the convention and started the Negro Baptist Convention of Texas. This convention retained the teachings of the Baptist faith, but it made the Baptist teachings applicable to the black race of America during that time. Until his death in 1915, Boyd worked hard to make the Black Baptist voice heard in hopes that it would endure after his time.

The first attempt to organize a local church in the city of Dixon, Illinois came shortly after 1866. The membership met in a frame dwelling located on Hennepin Avenue between Second and Third Street. No one really knows what happened, but the attempt to start a church was short-lived. In 1915, a second attempt was made. Under the leadership of Reverend Mayor Ashford, the church began to conduct meetings in the homes of its members. Two of its meeting locations were 606 Monroe Avenue and 516 West Sixth Street. The membership of sixteen people agreed upon the name "The Community Church" as the church's functional title. Once the church was incorporated, Reverend

Fletcher became its first part-time Pastor. Reverend Fletcher was formally recognized and subsequently recommended by the Ministerial Alliance and Northern Baptist Association.

In 1916, the young people of the church formed the "Equal Rights Social Club." The club began raising money in order to purchase a lot, for their meetings and eventual congregation, at 605 Madison Avenue in Dixon, IL. The cost of the lot was $300, and Mrs. Squires (the owner of the lot) donated the first $50.00. In 1919, Deacon Berry Steward and Mrs. Jennie Coleman hosted the club at their home, and in 1920, Mrs. Clara Thomas suggested that the church be built upon the lot at 1605 Madison Avenue. The club introduced a brick party and purchased bricks at $1.00 each. At some point during the actual construction of the building, the membership voted to change the name from the Community Church to the Second Baptist Church.

Reverend Lindell raised funds from Lee County citizens to fund the laying of the foundation and the construction of the walls for the new Second Baptist Church. Interest was carried on by Mrs. Flora McReynold, Mrs. Gladys, Peniston, Mrs. Victoria Dotson, Mrs. Alice Spotts, and Deacon Berry Stewart. In 1921 Deacon Berry Stewart, R.E. Buke, and George Collins announced that $1,000.00 had been spent toward the construction of the building. Many local citizens also donated funds to assist with the financial requirements of the church. Under Pastor Hawkins leadership, the building was completed by the end of 1921.

During an evening service in October 1923, the Ku Klux Klan (KKK) entered the sanctuary and presented Pastor Hawkins with an envelop containing four ten dollar bills. The congregation was informed that the Klan had observed the congregation's efforts regarding the construction of their own church and the KKK stated that their donation was offered to this black church in the spirit of Christ.

In December 1923, the church membership voted to release Pastor Hawkins of his duties. The deacons cited that the church needed the money that they were paying Pastor Hawkins to retire the mortgage. After the release of Pastor Hawkins, the following ministers contributed to the spiritual development of the church: Reverend A.W. Hawks, Reverend Trotter, Reverend Williams, Reverend Woods, Reverend Patton, Reverend Stamps, and Reverend Simmons.

In 1924, the church held a week-long revival: the guest minister was Reverend A.W. Nix from Chicago, Illinois. Rev. Nix served as a minister with the National Baptist Conference. Reverend Nix's opening sermon was entitled "Going to Hell – and Who Cares?" and his Reverend Nix's closing sermon was called "The Eagle Sirs Her Nest." Notably, in 1926, Reverend E.C. Williams preached a controversial sermon at the

Second Baptist Church entitled "Jazz or Jesus." In 1927, the church organized a four-day community revival; the purpose for this revival was to focus on the spiritual and moral issues of the city of Dixon, Illinois, and the guest minister was Dr. E.W. Hawthorn from Chicago, Illinois.

Under the leadership of Pastor Simmons, the Second Baptist Church remodeling project began. First on the agenda was to replace an old stove with a furnace. By 1946, a wooden floor replaced the concrete floor, two Sunday school rooms were added, the choir-stand and pulpit were renovated, cloak rooms were added, and the walls were painted. The Methodist church in Rochelle, Illinois donated chairs to replace the uncomfortable benches. In 1948 Reverend Clayborn Salters became the church's first full-time Pastor. Under Pastor Salters' leadership, the remodeling project was completed. The church finished painting the kitchen and installing telephones and modern plumbing facilities. Pastor Salters organized the Youth Department and Usher Board. The membership grew to sixty-one, and the church property was valued at $20,000. Other Pastors who contributed to the growth and development of the church after Pastor Salters were Pastor Charles Manney, Pastor Cleophas McKinzee, Pastor Percy Carter, and Pastor George Wright.

In 1956, Reverend Rudolph S. Shoultz became the church's second longest serving full-time Pastor.

Pastor Shoultz, a native of Jamaica, served as Associate Pastor of St. Paul Baptist Church in Freeport, Illinois. Under Pastor Shoultz leadership, the church doubled in size.

During a board meeting, the membership authorized the Trustee Board to begin searching for a larger building. On December 9, 1963 the church acquired the former church of the Brethren located at 501 Third Street. After spending $10,000 in renovation costs, the church moved into its new location on March 8, 1964.

Pastor Shoultz's legacy is remembered as fostering a better understanding between races. Pastor Shoultz served in many capacities on the local and state levels. Pastor Shoults was also appointed by Governor Otto Kerner to serve as committee member of the 1970 White House Conference on Children and Youth. In 1968, Pastor Shoultz resigned and assumed the pastoral leadership of the Union Baptist Church of Springfield, Illinois. Under the new leadership of Pastor Lundy Savage and Pastor Raymond Nash, the church retired its mortgage. A mortgage burning ceremony was held on September 14, 1973. The presiding minister was Pastor Shoultz.

In 1975, Reverend A.J. Downing became the next Pastor. Under Pastor Downing's leadership, two associate ministers accepted their calling as full-time Pastors. Pastor Downing increased the Second

Baptist Church's visibility by supporting the Senior Citizen Center, Open Sesame Day Care Center, and he supported various community programs. Reverend Downing served as Pastor until his death in 1983. Other Pastors who contributed to the growth and development of the church after Pastor Downing were; Pastor John Davidson and Pastor Jerry Porter. The current Pastor of Second Baptist Church is Reverend Galon Darby who began his ministry there in 1993. Reverend Darby is the longest serving full-time Pastor in Second Baptist history.

Under the leadership of Pastor Darby, the church purchased a sixteen-seat passenger van, remodeled the sanctuary, and bought musical equipment and audio equipment. Pastor Darby has positioned the church to become financially stable and spiritually equipped.

Second Baptist Church remains an active place of worship for the African community in Dixon, Illinois. It is presently located at 501 West 3rd Street in the city.

4

The Early Methodist Movement

The theology of the Lee African American Episcopal Church (AMEC) is consistent with the teachings of the Methodist faith. The Methodist church originated from within the Protestant separatist movement, a movement which arose in England with the goal of breaking away from the Church of England.

The early Methodist movement can be traced back to 1738 where John Wesley and his brother Charles Wesley were studying at the University of Oxford. Though both Wesley brothers were ordained ministers of the Church of England, they were barred from speaking in most of its pulpits because of their evangelistic methods. The Wesley brothers did not set out to create a new church; rather, they sought to begin several small faith-restoration groups within the Anglican community called the "United Societies." The Methodist teachings spread and eventually became its own separate denomination when the first conference was held in 1744. Subsequently, the AMEC grew out of the Free African Society (FAS) which Richard Allen, Absalom Jones, and other established leaders led in Philadelphia in 1787.

During a service at the St. George's Methodist Episcopal Church, blacks were pulled off their knees while praying. Because of that incident, the FAS members discovered how far the American Methodist would go to enforce racial discrimination against African Americans. The African American membership of St. George made plans to transform their mutual aid society into an African congregation. In 1794, Bethel AMEC was dedicated with Allen as their Pastor.

To establish Bethel's independence from interfering with white Methodist, Allen, a former Delaware slave, successfully sued in the Pennsylvania courts in 1807 and 1815 for the right of his congregation to exist as an independent institution. Because black Methodist in other middle Atlantic communities encountered racism and desired religious autonomy, Allen called them to meet in Philadelphia to form new Wesleyan denomination, the African Methodist Episcopal (AME).

The geographical spread of the AMEC prior to the Civil War was mainly restricted to the Northeast and Midwest. Major congregations were established in Philadelphia, New York, Boston, Pittsburgh, Baltimore, Washington DC, Cincinnati, Chicago, Detroit, and other large Blacksmith Shop cities. Numerous northern communities also gained a substantial AME presence. Remarkably, the states of Maryland, Kentucky, Missouri, Louisiana, and for a few years, South Carolina, became additional locations for AME congregations. The denomination reached Pacific Coast in the early 1850's with Mother Bethel Churches, in Stockton, Sacramento, San Francisco, and other places in California. Moreover, Bishop Morris Brown established the Canada Annual Conference.

The most significant era of denominational development occurred during the Civil War and Reconstruction. Oftentimes, with the permission of Union army official AME clergy moved into the states of the collapsing Confederacy to pull newly freed slaves into their denomination. "I Seek My Brethren," the title of an often repeated sermon that Theophilus G. Steward preached in South Carolina, became a clarion call to evangelize fellow blacks in Georgia, Florida, Alabama, Texas, and many other parts of the south. Hence, in 1880 AME membership reached 400,000 because of its spread below the Mason-Dixon line. When Bishop Henry M. Turner pushed African Methodism across the Atlantic into Liberia and Sierra Leone in 1891 and into South Africa in 1896, the AME laid claim to adherents on two continents.

While the AME is doctrinally Methodist, clergy scholars, and lay person have written important works which demonstrate the distinctive theology and praxis which have defined this Wesleyan body. Bishop Benjamin W. Arnett, in an address to the 1893 World's Parliament of Religions, reminded the audience of the presence of blacks in the formation of Christianity. Bishop Benjamin T. Tanner wrote in 1895 in the Color of Solomon - What? That biblical scholars wrongly portrayed the son of David as a white man.

In 1921, twelve residents from the City of Dixon Illinois met in the home of Mr. William Swain and organized the Lee African Methodist Episcopal Church (AMEC). No one really knows how the name "Lee" was decided upon, but it is believed that the name was determined by the county in which they lived. In 1922, the Reverend Spear was appointed the church's first Pastor. Currently, the AMEC Pastors are appointed yearly upon the recommendation of the presiding Elder and the Bishop; this appointment is normally decided during the church's annual conference. Pastors who were appointed at the Lee AMEC between 1923 and 1931 were Pastor Day, Pastor Pennington, Pastor Bass, Pastor Bryant, Pastor Peterson, Pastor Lee, Pastor Trotter, and Pastor Bell.

In 1924, Mrs. Luceal Randal (a local resident) donated a small building to the Lee AMEC Church. The church worshipped in the building for the next few years. Prior to the dedication service on Sunday, June 8, 1924, the church changed its name from the Lee AMEC to the Lee AME Mission. Mayor Frank D. Palmer gave the opening address. Letters from various local Pastors were read. The guest speaker was the Reverend Unangst, former Pastor of the Grace Evangelical Church. The service was well attended by white residents. Other high ranking AMEC officials who participated in the service were; Reverend J.M. Bracken and Reverend J.S. Woods from Chicago, Illinois. The Reverend Marchant from Rockford, Illinois also attended the service.

In 1932, Reverend Charles Enouch became Pastor of the Lee AME Mission. Under Pastor Enoch's leadership, the church voted to purchase the property at 509 Seventh Street. Through the efforts of Mrs. Luceal Randal the church purchased the property for $1,100. The original members of the church were Arthur Kadogan, William Swain, R.E. Burke, Charles Smith, Silas Smith, Wesley Ashford, Delena Kadogan, Ella Smith, Eva Cook Mack, Clara Young , and Mattie Goodman. The Trustees of the church were Arthur Kadogan, William Swain, and R.E. Burke. The stewards and stewardess were Charles Smith, Mattie Goodman, Wesley Ashford, Delena Kadogan, Mattie Swain, and Eva Cook Mack. In 1933, the Reverend E.A. Sappington became Pastor. On September 1, 1933, Reverend Sappington organized a Community Tag Day. The purpose for this day was to solicit donations from the community to assist with the financial obligations of the church.

On November 21, 1924, the church invited an African American student named Miss Wylna Fletcher from Knox College in Galesburg, Illinois to perform such songs as "Come unto Him" from Handel's Messiah and "I Talked to God Last Night." To accommodate seating, the concert was held at the First Christian Church of Dixon. In December 1950, the Reverend Charles Harry Peugh became Pastor of the Lee AME Mission. Under Pastor Peugh, the church membership grew to include the notable members Delena Kadogan, John Bell, Eitta Springfield, Bessie Pennington, Gene Ashford, Lillie Ashford, Maggie Ashford, Major Ashford, Zelodias Williams, Pauline Wisely, and Johnnie Wyatt Jones. In 1951, Pastor Peugh applied to the Dixon Chamber of Commerce for assistance in beautifying the church property.

On May 5, 1951, the church was informed that it had been selected to have the exterior of the church painted. The program was a part of Dixon, Illinois' "clean up week" campaign, and on May 7, 1951 members of Painters Union 1081 were selected for the job. The local union consisted of painters from the Dixon, Sterling, and Rock Falls area. The paint was donated by local merchants, and approximately forty to fifty painters participated; at the time of completion, the church held the distinguished title of being the only building in Dixon to be painted in two and a half hours.

In 1953, the Reverend Leonard Ashford became the church's next Pastor. Reverend Ashford served as Pastor between 1953 and 1957. In 1958, due to declining membership and financial hardship, the church closed its doors. However, In 1966, the church reopened its doors. The church changed its name from Lee A.M.E. Mission to Lee AME Chapel. The Reverend G. Paul Jones and Reverend Leonard Ashford were appointed Pastors. Reverend Jones also serves as Pastor for the St. James AMEC in Monmouth, Illinois.

The property became owned by Mrs. J.R. Raiston. Mrs. Raiston donated the property back to the church. Under the leadership of Pastor Jones and Pastor Ashford, plans were drawn to remodel the front of the church. On April 27, 1973, the church held a special service to honor its current Pastor, the Reverend J.H. Harris. Second Baptist Church of Dixon Illinois was the guest church and Pastor Raymond Nash delivered the sermon. On August 17, 1973, a memorial service was held for Pastor Leonard Ashford; Pastor Ashford was born in 1882 and spent most of his life in Dixon.

After 1973, no more information could be found concerning the activities of the Lee AME Chapel. According to the Dixon Assessment office, the property, located at 509 South Seventh Street remained in the name of Mr. Raiston until 1997. Between 1998 and 1999 Mrs. Zelodias Ashford owned the property. Between 2000 and 2001, Mrs. Carolyn Brooks owned the property. In 2002, Dixon Habitat for Humanity owned the property and sub-divided it into two lots, where residential homes are now present.

5

The Additional Methodist Center

The Worship Center is listed with the Dixon, Illinois Chamber of Commerce

The theology of The Worship Center is consistent with the theology of the Methodist faith. The Methodist church originated from within the Protestant separatist movement, a movement which arose in Europe with the goal of breaking away from the Church of England.

Those who founded the Christian Methodist Episcopal Church (CMEC) had been members of the Methodist Episcopal (ME) Church, South, while they were slaves. John Wesley and the early Methodists had opposed slavery. However, by 1830, the ME Church, organized in the famous Christmas Conference in 1784, had become a slave-holding church. In 1844, it split over the issue of slavery, as was true of many Protestant denominations in America. Methodists were very effective in preaching the Gospel of Jesus Christ to slaves. It was primarily through slaves that African

Americans heard the preaching of the Gospel and were converted to become followers of Jesus Christ and faithful Methodists. Many of the slaves were licensed to preach. In 1860, more than 207,000 slaves were members of the ME Church. At the close of the Civil War, more than 78,000 slaves were members.

Isaac Lane, a licensed minister within the ME Church, requested a separate and independent church for African Americans. According to Lane, "The preaching of the Gospel should be patterned after our ideas and notions." The General Conference of the ME Church, South agreed, and in 1866 during its annual meeting in New Orleans, the conference organizers granted Lane's request. On December 15, 1870, Lane and forty other ministers from the ME Church, South Convention met in Jackson, Tennessee and organized the Colored Methodist Episcopal Church (CMEC). During a general conference meeting in 1954, the conference organizers voted to change the name from "Colored" to "Christian" so that it came to be called the Christian Methodist Episcopal Church (CMEC).

In 1992, Reverend Michael Cole, Sr. and his wife Geraldine Cole from Freeport, Illinois were traveling evangelists with the CMEC. In August 1992, while traveling to Dixon, God spoke to Pastor Cole and charged him to commit to a permanent ministry in the City of Dixon. On November 29, 1992, the New Wine CME Mission was founded.

The Early Methodist Movement 71

The original membership of the church consisted of Michael Cole, Sr., Geraldine Cole (wife), Percyl Cole, Falecia Cole, Michael Cole, Jr., Debra Adams, Christopher Adams, and Chaz Josephson Adams. The first United Methodist Church of Dixon, Illinois allowed the membership to meet in the church Chapel. The church was located at 202 South Peoria Avenue.

During the CME annual conference on December 13, 1992, Reverend Haywood Henry (Presiding Elder) officially announced the church as the CME Missions of Dixon. Because the church was founded, a CME appointment was not needed. The church continued to worship at 202 South Peoria Avenue until November 1993. As the membership grew to approximately forty people, the leadership voted to purchase the property at 405 Keul Road. The property was purchased for $70,000. The property was previously owned by the Jehovah Witnesses. In December 1993, the Presiding Bishop decided to change the name from "New Wine CME Church" to "Ester Isom Worship Center CME Church"; The name was changed to recognize Bishop Dotcy Isom Jr., wife. To break away from a denominational title, on August 22, 2002, the leadership of the church voted to change the name from "Ester Isom Worship Center CME Church" to "The Worship Center."

The church purchased the property at 403 North Ottawa Street; this property was previously owned by the Church of Christ. Under the leadership of Pastor Cole, the church remodeled the sanctuary, purchased a passenger van, upgraded the restrooms for handicap accessibility, purchased a new sound system, purchased musical equipment, and created a web site.

Presently, the work known as, The Worship Center, is an active church under the direction of Pastor Cole. One of the active areas of ministry is The School of Love in Deliverance with an exciting and effective program known as S.O.L.I.D. It is a Christian based twelve-step program centered on the foundational precepts of the delivering power of Christ. A basic theme of the ministry is "We sing to an audience of One as we strive to become the Body of Christ through the unity of the Holy Spirit."

In giving rights to others which belong to
them, we give rights to ourselves
and to our country.

—John Fitzgerald Kennedy

> In social theory one learns that
> individuals change more rapidly than groups;
> groups faster than communities;
> communities easier than society
>
> — Hollis L. Green

6

The Prison Ministry Involvement

The Importance of Black Church Involvement

Since the number of African American adults behind prison bars is at an all time high it behooves the Black Church to minister to this growing prison population. African Americans are being incarcerated at an alarming rate. African Americans contribute to over half of the prison population in the United States. However, volunteerism from the black community is lacking. The black church has fallen short of establishing a relationship with the local law enforcement agency to determine what Chaplaincy service is available.

During my employment with the Illinois Department of Corrections at Dixon Correctional Center, I extended an invitation to the local community to assist the development of programs that would aid the incarcerated population. My department offered the local church an opportunity to grow in proportion to the incarcerated community. When the local church addresses the spiritual needs of its incarcerated membership, it fosters a positive change for the good of both inmates and the community. When that change occurs it fosters a strong faith based community that can also minister to the family of inmates.

The black community has an obligation to analyze the nature of the gospel of Jesus Christ in light of the prison population. Individuals incarcerated and their family members must see the church taking an active role in restoring each inmate not only to their family and church, but to the community at large. The Gospel and the various ministries of the church must be seen as part and parcel of the fabric of home that is held in the heart and mind of all inmates and their loved ones.

When ministering to those in prison, we must not conclude that all incarcerated persons are guilty of a crime. The black church must teach self-respect and self-esteem in spite of social and political hardship. Wrongdoing must never be justified, but wrongdoers must never be condemned. The message of saving grace must be presented in love and with compassion to anyone who will hear. Since faith can move mountains, surely faith is strong enough to breach the walls of a prison and set souls free from the law of sin and death.

The first biblical reference of "prison," is when Joseph was placed in a cistern by his brothers (Gen.

37:23 & 24). This cistern became Joseph's place of incarceration. Joseph was placed there because of the jealousy of his brothers. He had not wronged them or done anything offensive to anybody. Can you just imagine travelers passing by that way, seeing Joseph in that cistern-prison and concluding he was there because he deserved to be! That would have been tragic and, yet, we do the same thing when we see someone under arrest, in jail or in prison. We almost automatically conclude they deserve to be there.

In the gospel according to Matthew, the writer records that it was at the decisive moment of John the Baptist's imprisonment that prompted Jesus to move out in His ministry. Imprisonment may be the motivating factor to inspire the local church to engage in ministry. It can also be a time of decision when God finally has the inmate's total attention. Prison can be a moment of decision for drastic change in behavior and lifestyle. Families can be put back together. God is still in the "fixing business."

When the Black Church understands the guidelines listed below they can have an effective prison ministry:

1. Inform the church body of their biblical obligation to minister to persons who are incarcerated.

2. Pray that individual members be brought under conviction to participate in prison ministry.

3. Contact your local law enforcement agency to find out how the church may minister to persons in their custody.

4. Pray that God will use each one who makes a commitment to work in the prison ministry.

5. Always report to the church the "victories" experienced in the process of encountering inmates.

6. Follow-up on all promises made to inmates.

7. Always be a Christian example before those you encounter as part of the prison ministry.

I am a success today because I had a friend who believed in me and I didn't have the heart to let him down.

—Abraham Lincoln

> There are those who say to you - we are rushing this issue of civil rights. I say we are 172 years late.
>
> — Hubert H. Humphrey

7

The Fight for Justice Continues

Frederick Douglass

Thomas J. Fearer of Pine Creek Township in Ogle County, Illinois wrote in his dairy that he was mounting his horse to travel to Dixon, Illinois to hear Frederick Douglass speak. Douglass, a famous leader of the abolitionist movement, fought to end slavery. Douglass was asked by the Anti-Slavery Society to engage in a tour of lectures, and he became recognized as one of America's first great black speakers. Douglass won world attention when his autobiography was published in 1845. Two years later, he began publishing an antislavery paper called "The North Star." Woodbridge N. Ferris of Freeport, Illinois wrote in his autobiography that, "In Dixon I heard Frederick Douglass lecture on the subject of 'Self-Made Man.' He read from a manuscript and when half through stopped suddenly, closed his book and without explanation left the platform." It seems that people were not listening with sufficient intensity to satisfy his total commitment to the cause. It appears that there are not half-measures when one is fighting for justice.

Daybreak of Duty

Duty and personal responsibility began to shed light on the problem of inequality when President Lincoln signed the Emancipation and the brave generalship of President Grant pressed for legal action to project the slaves freed by the Civil War. The American duty became clear: time was running out on slavery and racial discrimination. Regardless of how hard the bigots tried they could not put God's swift lightning back in a box or hold back the incoming tide of surging hope.

Douglass Supported Grant

In 1868, Douglass supported the presidential campaign of Ulysses S. Grant. President Grant signed into law the Klan Act and the second and third Enforcement Acts. Grant used their provisions vigorously, suspending habeas corpus in South Carolina and sending troops there and into other states; under his leadership, over 5,000 arrests were made and the Ku Klux Klan received a serious blow. Grant's vigor in disrupting the Klan made him unpopular among many whites, but Frederick Douglass praised him. An associate of Douglass wrote of Grant that African Americans "will ever cherish a grateful remembrance of his name, fame and great services."

What One Determined Man Could Do

Douglass continued to participate vigorously in the affairs of state and demonstrate what one determined man could do for the cause of justice. After the Civil War, he was appointed to several important political positions. He served as President of the Reconstruction-era Freedman's Savings Bank; as marshal of the District of Columbia; as minister-resident and consul-general to the Republic of Haiti (1889–1891); and as chargé d' affaires for the Dominican Republic. After two years, he resigned from his ambassadorship because of disagreements with U.S. government policy. In 1872, he moved to Washington, D.C., after his house on South Avenue in Rochester, New York burned down; arson was expected.

A Flicker of Light

Those who sat in the darkness of despair saw a flicker of light. The gaze of preceding generations had fixed a hope on the coming deliverance. The twilight of intolerance was eclipsed by the dark bigotry of segregation, but beneath the despair of the people was the slumbering force of an indestructible hope. It was time for the "true Light" to penetrate the night and to point the way to equality. For many years, wise men had searched the limits of human knowledge and probed the unlimited reaches of their souls for a sign to guide them in their quest for justice. The day came when Dr. King said, "I Have a Dream!" Since that day, the dream has been carried to the uttermost part of the United States of America, the shadows of despair are lifting, and there is hope in the land.

African Liberation had Setbacks

Liberation of African Americans is more sacred today than ever before, because history points to many set-backs along the journey to justice. White insurgents quickly arose in the South after the Civil War. In spite of President Grant's efforts to protect the freed slaves, the white south organized vigilante groups such as the Ku Klux Klan. They took different forms through the years; the last was powerful paramilitary groups such as the White League and the Red Shirts during the 1870s in the Deep South. Their power grew in the South after Reconstruction, leading to white Democrats' regaining political power after the Civil War in every state of the former Confederacy and reasserting white supremacy. They enforced this by a combination of violence, new laws imposing segregation and a concerted effort to disfranchise African Americans. They passed new state constitutions and statutes in the South from 1890-1908 that created requirements for voter registration and voting that effectively disfranchised most of the poor. This disfranchisement and segregation were enforced for more than six decades into the 20th century.

Reflecting the Face of America

Prophecies of the Bible can only be applied to real life when the problems of the people are addressed. Nothing can ever erase the historical significance of the black church in the City of Dixon and elsewhere; although the black church has become multicultural and diverse there is still a distance to travel before total equality is assured. As the faith community continues to embrace the theology of one Lord, one faith, and one baptism, the worshipers in Dixon, Illinois have reflected the face of America; no longer are they separated as a religious community, but they are united in the bond of peace. The big question: Will the City of Dixon ever achieve Dr. Martin Luther King's dream concerning all of God's people (black and white, Jews and gentiles, Protestants, and Catholics) joining hands together? Yes, we pray and work that in time it will happen. Much has been done to eradicate injustice, but there is a long way to journey before the night ends and the Day Star arises.

Hopefully, this journey will include more interaction between the various churches and more cooperation among the various people who live, work, and worship in Dixon, Illinois. This may have been Dr. King's dream, but it is our reality and by faith we claim the truth that God has created all equal before the bar of Justice.

If man hasn't discovered something that he will die for, he isn't fit to live.

—Martin Luther King, Jr.

> A minority cannot protect itself against the violence imposed by discrimination, injustice, or prejudice.
>
> —Hollis L. Green

About the Author

Professional Service

- 27 years with the Illinois Department of Corrections
- 25 years of part-time teaching with the State Board of Education
- 10 years with the Dixon Police Department
- 7 years with the Sterling Police Department
- 5 years with Katherine Shaw Bethea Hospital

Academic Achievements

- Bachelor of Science in Music Education from Southern Illinois University in Carbondale.
- Master of Divinity from Anchor Theological Seminary in Edinburg, Texas.
- Doctorate of Ministry in Christian Philosophy from Anchor Theological Seminary in Edinburg, Texas.
- Elementary and Secondary teacher's certifications from the Illinois State Board of Education in Springfield Illinois.

- Ordination certification with:
  a. American Baptist Churches, USA
  b. National Baptist Convention, USA
  c. Illinois State Association of Police Chaplains

Historical Accomplishments

- Commissioner for the City of Dixon Arts and Community Affairs.
- Auxiliary Police Officer for the City of Dixon Police Department.
- Senior Chaplain for the Dixon Correctional Center.
- District Chaplain for the Illinois Department of Corrections.
- Chaplain for the Sterling Police Department.
- Chaplain for Katherine Shaw Bethea Hospital.

Appendix One:

Book Logo Data

The Logo Colors

The logo for this book was designed to show that both black and white churches can work together and augment pure religion in the community. Black and white colors were chosen because they can augment, supplement, enhance, and enlarge the religious community. In reality black and white, as a description, is a misnomer because these colors contain shades of gray. Yet each has distinct characteristics to bring to the mix in spite of human failings.

Although black is a mysterious color associated with fear and the unknown, black also denotes strength and authority and is associated with power, elegance, formality, and mystery. White is associated with light, goodness, innocence, and is considered the color of perfection. White means safety, purity, and cleanliness and usually has a positive connotation.

The Squares

The Squares are black and white and have four equal sides and four right angles. The four sides represent equality: personal, social, spiritual and racial. There are three squares in the logo: one black and two white. These represent the structured or established churches that should work together in fellowship to advance commonalities of religious faith. It is common ground, not differences, that advance knowledge and understanding.

The Cross

The Cross was an early symbol of Christianity. The shape of the cross made no difference. The cross in the logo is an interwoven X-shaped cross, commonly called the St. Andrew's Cross Named for Simon Peter's brother, Andrew, who was martyred by crucifixion on an X-shaped cross at his own request, because he deemed himself unworthy to be crucified in the same manner as Christ. The X-shaped cross signifies his resolution or resolve. The X is interwoven with the square representing the church and with itself representing the integration of basic Christianity.

The Fish

The fish symbol occurred early in Christian history and was placed in the center of the cross. After the crucifixion believers were persecuted and the fish became a symbol Christians would recognize, but others would not. Therefore, believers could connect through this symbol without being exposed to their oppressors. The Greek word for fish, ΙΧΘΥΣ, was used as an acrostic to advance the Christian faith. The Greek letters for fish were given the meaning "Jesus Christ God's Son Savour" to the early believers. They also saw the X-shaped cross in the tail of the fish. The FISH symbol was placed in the center of the cross to represent a central concept in religion.

All, too, will bear in mind this sacred principle, that though the will of the majority is in all cases to prevail, that will, to be rightful, must be reasonable; that the miniority possess their equal rights, which equal laws must protect, and to violate would be oppression.

—Thomas Jefferson

Appendix Two

The Commonality of the Golden Rule

Buddhism

Hurt not others in ways that you yourself would find hurtful.

    Udana-Varga 5,1

Christianity

As you would that men should do unto you, do you also to them likewise.

    Luke 8:31

Confucianism

Do not do to others what you would not like yourself. Then there will be no resentment against you, either in the family or in the state.

    Analects 12:2

Hinduism

This is the sum of duty; do naught onto others what you would not have them do unto you.

    Mahabharata 5,1517

Islam

No one of you is a believer until he desires for his brother that which he desires for himself.

    Sunnah

Judaism

What is hateful to you, do not do to your fellowman. This is the entire Law; all the rest is commentary.

    Talmud, Shabbat 3id

Taoism

Regard your neighbor's gain as your gain, and your neighbor's loss as your own loss.

    Tai Shang Kan Yin P'ien

Zoroastrianism

That nature alone is good which refrains from doing another whatsoever is not good for itself.

    Dadisten-I-dinik, 94,5

Appendix Three:

Sources Listed By Date

(1919 – 2008)

Colored Baptist Church. (1919, November 20). *The Evening Telegraph* [Dixon, Il]. P8.

Dixon Klan gives to colored church last eve. (1923, October 15). *The Evening Telegraph* [Dixon, Il]. P1.

Dispense with Pastor. 1923, December 29). *The Evening Telegraph* [Dixon, Il]. P2.

To dedicate colored church here Sunday. (1924, June 6) *The Evening Telegraph* [Dixon, Il]. P1.

A.M.E. Mission dedicated Sunday P.M. (1924, June 9). *The Evening Telegraph* [Dixon, Il]. P2.

Bloodshed is outcome of a church quarrel. (1933, March 7). *The Evening Telegraph* [Dixon, Il] P1.

Tag Day Tomorrow. (1933, September 1). *The Evening Telegraph* [Dixon, Il].P1

Lee A.M.E. Mission will sponsor singer. (1942, November 21). *The Evening Telegraph* [Dixon, Il]. P3

Lee A.M.E. Church organized by congregation 29 years ago. (1951, May 1). *The Evening Telegraph* [Dixon, Il]. Centennial Edition: P6.

Painters marathon will refinish this building. (1951, May 5). *The Evening Telegraph* [Dixon, Il]. P1.

Painters give A.M.E. church 'face-lifting' in two-and- a-half hours. (1951, May 7). *The Evening Telegraph* [Dixon, Il]. P1.

Second Baptist will move to new building on Sunday. (1964, March 7). *The Evening Telegraph* [Dixon, Il], P4.

Community Center to be Rejuvenated. (1966, July 15). *The Evening Telegraph* [Dixon, Il]. P6.

Set service at Lee Chapel A.M.E. Church. (1966, September 2). *The Evening Telegraph* [Dixon, Il]. P6.

Reverend Shoultz is Leaving. (1968, February 8). *The Evening Telegraph* [Dixon, Il]. P9.

Sunday Honorees. (1973, April 27). *The Evening Telegraph* [Dixon, Il]. P3.

Second Baptist Movement dates to 1866. (1976, February 28). The Evening Telegraph [Dixon, Il]. Heritage Edition: section G10.

First blacks came in 1866; church began in 1915.(1978, February 25) The Evening Telegraph [Dixon, Il].P2.

African Methodist Episcopal Church. (2008, November 10). http;//www.ame-church.com/about-us/history.php

Methodist Church – Brief History of Methodist Denomination. (2008. November 6). Christianity. about.com/od/ Methodistdenomination/a/ methodishistory.htm-22k

Richard Henry Boyd. 2008, September 6). www.tnstate. edu/library/digital/RHBoyd.htm-5k

Baptist History. (2008, October 14) www.yellowstone.net/ baptist/history. htm-31k

Appendix Three: Sources Listed by Date

African Methodist Episcopal Church. (2008, November 10). http://www.ame-church/about-us/history.php

Methodist Church - Brief History of the Methodist Denomination. (2008). Christianity. about.com/od/Methodistdenomination/a/methodishistoryhtm-22k

History of the Christian Methodist Episcopal (CME) Church. (2008. November 1) http://www.godonthe.net/cme/history/cme-hist.htm

Cole, Michael. Personal interview. (2008, November 6).

Notes

Notes

Notes

www.ingramcontent.com/pod-product-compliance
Lightning Source LLC
LaVergne TN
LVHW051847080426
835512LV00018B/3118